RELATIONSHIP SEASONS

FRANCINE QUAICOE

ENDORSEMENT

This book is an interesting read and worth having in your collections! It provides insight on how past traumas can impact adult relationships.
Thank you, Francine, for sharing this book with me. It is definitely an eye opener and has helped me reflect on my own personal life.
I also enjoyed reflecting on some of the questions and activities within Relationship Seasons. It allows for deeper conversations to take place and different perspectives on relationships.
Thank you, once again, for all your support, advice, and guidance!

Robert James Christian, Spokenword Artist

CONTENTS

RELATIONSHIP SEASONS

PROLOGUE

Reflection
Am I infatuated or was it a distraction?
When it came to men, you were my 'hot selection.'
Now, I am starting to question your intention.
Was it even real?
I know we never signed the deal.
But I needed you like how I need a meal.

I remember we started to drift in November.
You went cold and it wasn't even winter.
I was critical.
Felt like there was someone in the picture.
So, I blocked you.
Then re-added you.
But all this back and forth was never in my character.

My feelings were deep like an ocean.
You never tried to swim; you were 'taking precaution.'
I kept telling myself, everything happens for a reason.
Upon reflection, you were just a lesson.
Like the weather, you were inconsistent.
When I needed you, you were moving distant.

So, I distant myself to get my mind back on track.
But anytime I moved on, you kept running back.
Repeatedly, you would say you wanted me, like, I was your crack.
Can't lie, I was addicted.
You said our 'art' could never die; it felt cremated.
The biggest L was I took your words to heart, but you took it for granted.
Funny thing is my intuition was right, even though you constantly denied it.
Lesson learnt, never give your heart to someone who hasn't earnt it.

1

LOVE & RELATIONSHIPS

Before speaking on love and relationships, it is important to first understand the origins of the term. The Bible describes love as "patient" and "kind."

"It does not envy, it does not boast, it is not proud. It does not dishonor others, it is not self-seeking, it is not easily angered, and it keeps no record of wrongs. Love does not delight in evil but rejoices with the truth. It always protects, always trusts, always hopes, and always perseveres."

(1 CORINTHIANS 13:4-7).

This definition is a perfect description of God's love. His love is steadfast and long-standing even when we are undeserving. This is the kind of love Paul challenges Christians to have.

Undoubtedly, love is a fundamental characteristic of who God is. The Bible states that "love is of God" and "God is love" (1 John 4:7–8). In other words, everything God does is impelled and influenced by His love. Thus, because love originated from God and His entire essence is cemented by love, we have the potential and capability to demonstrate this gift unto others (since we are made in His image) - "the LORD God formed man of the dust of the ground and breathed into his nostrils the breath of life; and man became a living being" (Genesis 2:7).

The diversity of love is beautifully described in the Bible. We celebrate a range of different types of love. For example, Eros love (which comes from the term erotic, passionate love). This type of love is manifested in the relationship between Solomon and Shulamite; Philia love (love of friends and equals) this is demonstrated in the deep friendship between David and Johnathan; Storge love (love of parents and children) shown in the fatherly love of Paul for Timothy, and, of course, Agape love (love of mankind) reinforced in the sacrificial, saving love of Christ for the elect.

These examples suggest individuals possess Godly attributes in terms of demonstrating and receiving love. We must therefore measure our expectation and experience based on Biblical standards rather than worldly perceptions. This is because the world offers a weak, flawed, and incomplete definition of the word - leading to confusion, inaccuracy, and unrealistic goals. To affirm whether we practice self-love or love within our own personal relationships, we must first ask ourselves:

- Do I exercise patience?
- Do I keep track of wrong doings?
- Do I practice forgiveness?

Some people may argue that love has lost its meaning and significance in modern society. We no longer place value on relationships. Rather, priority is given to egocentrism and materialism - such as wealth, prestige, and status. Whilst this may be justifiable to some extent, Abraham Maslow, founder of humanistic psychology, argues this can lead to toxicity and discontentment. Why? Because human beings were born to love and engage in fruitful relationships. It is part of our DNA. Maslow (1943) postulated that individuals were driven by an innate desire to be happy and reach self-actualisation. To do so, there were several prerequisites that had to be met − 'love and belonging' being one of them. This emotional and psychological need for interpersonal relationships, solidarity and intimacy were essential ingredients for individuals to live fulfilled and complete lives. This stance was supported by philosopher Immanuel Kant who also agreed that individuals were on a journey to reach the 'summum bonum' − the highest good.

Maslow stressed in order to reach the 'highest good', the basic needs which needed to be addressed were "physiological", "safety", "belonging and love", "social needs" or "esteem", and "self-actualization". This is best described in his hierarchy of needs (see image A) where he highlights intimate relationships as integral for the enhancement of human co-existence. It is the oxygen for survival. Social psychologist, Roy Baumeister, also pointed out that the 'need to belong' is one of the main forces that drives individuals. Thus, if love and relationships were necessary for human development, one can argue that it is probable for God to equip individuals with the tools and willingness to cultivate healthy relationships. After all, He breathed Himself (Love) unto us.

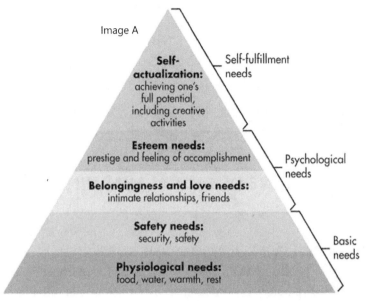

Dr. Phelan, *I Presume?* 2014

DISCUSSION
Based on Maslow's 'hierarchy of needs', what are the implications of toxic relationships on an individual's health and wellbeing?

....

....

....

....

....

....

....

2

SIGNS OF GLOBAL WARNING

Critiques, however, may question why some individuals find it difficult to forge healthy and positive relationships. Surely, if it is within our biological makeup, it should be straightforward and not limited to one's upbringing, gender, or religious background. This begs the question as to whether the ability to love is innate or nurtured by our environment.

It is comforting to believe the latter to be true. If individuals are products of their environment, it means no one was born a sadist. Rather, a blank piece of paper with society's fingerprints or written permission on it. This written document becomes a manuscript representing one's life (are you happy with your 'book' or does it require 'editing'?).

To put into context, there are some individuals that are simply toxic. Dealing with them can be frustrating and emotionally draining. Ever wondered what causes these people to be toxic? Were they born like that, or did they develop those traits from society?

Biological psychologists examine the relationship between mind, body, and heredity. According to this approach, behaviour is a consequence of our genetics and physiology. This means all thoughts, feelings and behaviour have a biological cause.

With that being said, toxic behavioral traits can be scientifically explained. For instance, Narcissistic Personality Disorder (NPD) is a cluster B personality disorder whereby individuals have an inflated sense of ego and a deep need for admiration. The origin of the name comes from a Greek myth, in which a hunter called Narcissus saw his reflection in a pool of water and fell in love with it. This excessive feeling of superiority and admiration trickles down into relationships forming unhealthy and toxic bonds.

What makes individuals vulnerable to this type of disorder? This is an interesting question. Yet, there are no conclusive answers. Though the cause for NPD remains a mystery, research have pointed out that narcissism is usually connected with a family medical history linked to mental health or a result of traumatic experience. In addition, research into the brain scan of narcissism shows less brain matter in areas associated with emotional empathy. This suggests NPD is biologically determined.

However, as a Sociologist, I take a more societal

approach to behavior. It is my opinion that NPD is a byproduct of societal influence - stemming from primary and secondary socialization. According to research, negative childhood experiences, such as being rejected or criticized by parents, can contribute to NPD in adulthood. At the same time, too much praise and pampering from parents can also lead to NPD.

In summary, it is clear that genetics is the bullet whilst society is the trigger. Meaning, NPD is caused by both genetics and environmental factors (e.g., child-parent relationship). Individuals with a family history linked to NPD are more likely to develop narcissistic traits if exposed to toxic childhood upbringing. As expected, this condition can cause friction within romantic relationships due to issues with empathy and intimacy.

However, it is important to avoid diagnosing individuals without any form of medical assessment. Just because your partner displays coldness or emotional unavailability does not mean they qualify as a narcissist. Healthcare professionals diagnose individuals based on their ability to display five characteristic traits.

1. Grandiose sense of importance
2. Fantasies of unlimited success
3. Haughty behaviors/attitudes
4. Excessive need for admiration

5. Lack of empathy

Whilst NPD is an interesting disorder that can be confusing, individuals with this type of condition can be a magnetic and highly skilled at attracting people. Their charm can be seductive, their charisma can light up a room, and their confidence can be comforting, (which is why so many people fall into the trap of dating them). To avoid being seduced by their charm, it is important to detect "global warnings" earlier on in the relationship. Marianne Vicelich, a self-love therapist, relationship coach and the author of twelve published self-help books, highlighted traits that were notably identifiable by narcissist (see following page).

1)   Projection

Have you ever dated someone that would constantly accuse you of doing something without any logical or tangible evidence? For example, they may accuse you of cheating. In turn, you end up jumping through hoops to prove your innocence only to find out they were the ones being unfaithful.

In my previous encounter with someone, the individual demonstrated his distrust towards me. Naively, I would bend over backwards to prove to him that I was genuine – only to find out he was sleeping with my 'friend'. This is a psychological trick whereby the narcissist projects blame unto their partner to mask their own behaviour.

In circumstances like this, it is best to remain headstrong and avoid proving anything to anyone. If a potential partner has difficulties trusting you (without any legitimate reason), they are under no obligation to remain with you.

2)   Emotionally Cold

Those with NPD are shallow with their emotions. During arguments, they shut down, withdraw, or respond in a cold manner. This can lead to the person at the receiving end becoming confused and attempting to generate warmth by chasing them.

In situations like this, it is best (and more productive) to chase yourself. Practice self-care and self-love. In practical sense, this looks like, developing your skill set, finding a hobby, engaging in meaningful projects. The list is endless. Whatever you do, it is important to find ways to empower and add value to your life.

3)   Gaslighting

From a historical perspective, the term arose from the 1930's play Gas Light, where a husband, to drive his wife crazy, keeps turning down the gas-powered lights in the house. When the wife asks why he is dimming the lights, he denies it and says they are no dimmer. Over time, she finds herself going mad.

"Gaslighting qualifies as a form of emotional abuse that involves denying a person's experience and making statements, such as 'that never happened' or 'you are too sensitive," Vicelich says. "The gaslighter uses techniques such as withholding or stonewalling, contradicting, or diversion, when you bring up something that concerns you. They also minimise your feelings and denies events that occurred. The consequence of gaslighting is that it leads to confusion, questioning your own reality and constantly apologising.

Although I am a strong advocate for self-reflection, taking accountability and apologising when required, it is equally important to avoid over apologising as this is fuel for the narcissist. Rather, a change of behaviour is an effective approach which can generate better results.

Nonetheless, if you realise gaslighting is a common occurrence within your relationship, it is best to avoid bowing down to the perpetrator's version of reality. Rather, practice saying; "the way I feel is not up to debate", "we clearly remember things differently, let's agree to disagree", "my truth is different regardless of what you say", "I have heard your viewpoint, but I still disagree". That way, you show the perpetrator that you are unwilling to submit to their delusion.

4)   Controlling

The term 'control freak' gets thrown around a lot, but what makes the situation even more frustrating is that often the narcissist controls you while remaining completely disinterested in the other aspects of your life. Vicelich explains that "control is … when a person feels like they cannot move without asking for permission. The narcissist uses control to isolate the person". For example, a partner may monitor your whereabouts, check your emails/text messages, criticise your appearance, and make nearly all-important decisions, with little regard for your opinion."

If these examples seem far too familiar or you feel micromanaged within your relationship, my best advice is to leave. Of course, that is easier said than done. In that case, set boundaries and consequences, avoid *internalising the criticism, seek counselling and, most importantly, ask for God's intervention.*

5) Lovebombing

Love bombing is the practice of overwhelming someone with adoration and attention in hope to gain trust and build themselves as the perfect partner. By doing so, the narcissist puts on a mask that their target will find admirable. They use strategies aimed to manipulate and remind their target of how much 'chemistry' they have. This is often the first line used by a potential abuser. It is used to keep their victims tethered.

SOLUTION BASED ACTIVITY

a) Identify signs of global warning (red flags) in your partner.
b) How it makes you feel (or how it effects your relationship)
c) Ways to overcome them.

You can do this with your partner or by yourself.

3

NIGHT & DAY

There is a common trend saying that these "h*** ain't loyal" and females echoing the same belief. The growing distrust amongst men and women is a major concern in modern culture. It can lead to sologamy, homosexuality and disrespect towards members of the opposite sex. This inevitably interrupts the natural flow of the universe as humans are designed to procreate.

However, just as "day" and "night" contributes to an entire day - men and women also contributes to a relationship. In other words, we need both "day" and "night" for the 24 hours to be complete. Similarly, we need both men and women present (or masculine and feminine energy) for a relationship to work.

Each have their own unique function. For instance, daytime provides light and heat. During this time, crops grow, and people work. Whereas, night-time is when the sun goes down, the sky becomes dark, and the moon is visible. During this time, people rest. For both "day" and "night" to experience its natural cause, the earth needs to rotate around the Sun.

Likewise, both genders have their own unique function contributing to a healthy relationship. Polarity in relationships sparks chemistry between opposing energies: masculine and feminine. It is important to note, gender does not affect whether you have masculine or feminine energies. Masculinity and femininity are spiritual concepts that involves energy. It is not synonyms for man and woman. All men have feminine energies, and all women have masculine energies. Energetic fields are subject to choice. Couples can be in a homosexual or heterosexual relationship, but for the pairing to work, one partner must provide the masculine polarity while the other brings the feminine polarity. Masculine energies (typically, men) are designed to be focused, and directive. They are most fulfilled when they have a purpose and are working towards a goal. Whereas feminine polarity seeks emotional fulfilment and connection. This type of energy is open, communicative, and nurturing.

Those with feminine energies are attracted to individuals with assertiveness and leadership skills. It makes them feel safe. Dr. Adrianne R. Pinkney (2018) mentioned, 'women feel more feminine in the presence of a masculine man'. Thus, 'his masculinity defines her femininity, and her femininity actually defines his masculinity'.

*She loves your hard arms because they
remind her that she is soft. When you lead by
creating a plan for the date, she is able to
feel at ease. She craves your protection
because it makes her feel precious.*

Whereas masculine energies 'gravitate towards those who appear to be receptive, nurturing, and passive' *(ibid)*.

The reason why some relationships may lack is because there are no polarities within the relationship. In other words, dysfunctional relationships can be traced back to depolarization, which is when one or both partners feel the need to develop the traits of the opposite energy. When a relationship depolarizes, the connection weakens. This occurs when both parties develop the same type of energy (e.g., masculine-masculine) or when they do not embrace their true selves.

In my previous relationship, I adopted the masculine role. Although my ex-partner was nice, loving, and kind, at times, I did not feel he possessed masculine attributes. Consequently, I found myself being the one who wore the trousers. This impacted our relationship as I could not submit myself to him. When I decided to 'take off the trousers', it felt like a feminine-feminine relationship. It could not work.

Upon reflection, I realised we both contributed to the problem. As a career woman, I spend a lot of time in my masculine energy (even though my core energy is feminine). I enjoy managing projects and planning affairs. In order to 'switch gears', I would need a masculine man to lead and direct. Masculinity is made powerful by what a 'man' does. In other words, masculine men are *doers*. He must first do for himself before he can pursue. Hence why one of the first questions women ask is, 'what do you *do*?' If you cannot answer the question, you have nothing to offer her. This has been the case since the beginning of time. In Ancient Kingdoms, no man had a wife until he did something to prove himself worthy. He had to complete a rite of passage, build a hut, and catch some type of animal to feed himself (and her).

In summary, a man remains in his masculinity when he is doing. This means he asks her out (initiating), plans the date (leadership), gives her compliments (assertive/confidence), holds the door (support), cuts some wood (capable), builds a house (protection/provision), works (active), and fertilizes an egg (creating).

Since my ex-partner had a laidback approach during the primitive stages of us dating, I automatically became the initiator. I would often plan dates and speak to him assertively. In turn, he became submissive. This dulled the relationship as I could not respect his manhood. To attract feminine women, you cannot live in your feminine energy. Likewise, to attract masculine men, you cannot live in your masculinity. In practical sense, this means if you want him to plan a special night for you, do not plan it. Request what you want and wait. Let him do. Be still. You can either drive or ride. There cannot be two drivers.

Shortly after, I started dating someone who, from the outlook, displayed masculine traits. I felt 'safe' around him and immediately became drawn to his energy. This highlights the fact that similar energies repel each other, whilst opposites attract. Two people with similar energies can love each other, but they can never have passion. It is therefore important to identify your core energy so that you can discern which polarity you are most compatible with.

Besides professional reasons, some people wear masks to avoid getting hurt. For example, those with feminine energies may wear a masculine mask to protect themselves from abuse or being taken advantage of. Underneath the mask, their innate energy does not change. To make the law of polarity work, it is important to strip away the mask and embrace your natural self.

However, this comes with self-confidence - a deep conviction that you are fearfully and wonderfully made (Psalms 139:14). It is important to note that God was intentional with His creation. He did not mistakenly create women to be emotional. Nor did He mistakenly create men to be sexual. It is there to serve a purpose. Once you discover your purpose, you can excel in your natural energy without fear of rejection or the need for validation.

Nevertheless, a woman who lives predominately in her masculine energy, is in 'protective mode'. She has built walls of masculinity due to emotional pain. This armor of protection is projected in a 'bad b****' mentality where she prioritises independence, ambition, and purpose. Although being independent is not inherently bad, hyper-independence can be seen as a trauma response resulting from being let down by others.

By understanding your identity and purpose, you begin to break free from this trauma mindset. This can only happen when you rotate around the "Sun". In simple terms, by making God the centerpiece of your life. This is because we are made in His image. He is the Author of our life. Therefore, we must seek guidance from the One that created us. Once you understand your uniqueness, you not only empower yourself, but you can be an addition to your partner. However, it does not stop there. God still needs to be the forefront of your union once unified with your spouse. Why? This is because "God is Love." Therefore, it makes sense to rotate around "Love" to truly experience and display *love*. Anything outside of that is subject to heartbreak.

Despite this, there seems to be an unspoken fear towards members of the opposite sex. It appears both men and women are afraid to be vulnerable and authentic due to trust issues. There is also a misconception amongst females that men are incapable of maintaining healthy Eros relationships as they do not possess the emotional intelligence or skills necessary for romantic relationships. This conception is flawed. Using pure logic, if men did not have the skills necessary for a romantic relationship, there would be no striving marriages. Why would God create individuals that could not love? Wouldn't that defeat His purpose?

To defend advocates with negative opinions of men or those that struggle to maintain healthy relationships, it may derive from personal experience or family dynamics. Due to an increase in single parent households, many are exposed to fatherless homes. The absence of father figures means children lack the benefits of having a healthy masculine energy in the home. This can lead to insecure attachment styles as children need a dependable adult to forge secure bonds. Sadly, single parent households (usually headed by women) do not have the privilege of having both parents. With fathers being absent, children are left broken.

John Bowlby, a psychiatrist, developed a premise called the attachment style theory. He believed that children were programmed to connect with others. The quality of bonding they receive during childhood determines how well they respond to intimacy in adulthood. Bowlby identified four types of attachment styles:

1. Secure Attachment
2. Anxious-ambivalent Attachment
3. Avoidant Attachment
4. Fearful Avoidant Attachment

1. Secure Attachment

The secure attachment style signifies a warm and loving bond between a parent and a child. The child feels cared for and loved. Those with secure attachment styles carry this healthy way of bonding into adulthood.

They have no problems building long-term relationships without fear of abandonment. These individuals are also comfortable expressing emotions openly. They do not base their self-worth or identity on relationships.

2. Anxious-Ambivalent Attachment

Anxious-ambivalent children tend to distrust their caregivers due to `inconsistent parenting, over protectiveness or emotional distance. They become emotionally dependent adults. The thought of living without their partner (or being alone) stresses them.

These types of people value their relationships highly. They tend to be insecure, clingy, and desperate for love. The attention and responsiveness of their partner seems to be the 'remedy' for their anxiety.

3. Avoidant Attachment

Children who have developed under the 'avoidant' style have learnt to accept that their emotional needs are likely to remain unmet. They continue to grow up feeling unloved and insignificant. As adults, they struggle with expressing their feelings and tend to avoid intimate relationships. These types of people can be described as 'lone wolves': strong, independent, and self-sufficient'. They are content being single and have difficulties depending on others.

4. Fearful- avoidant Attachment

This is when the child's caregiver who is supposed to be the primary source of safety becomes a source of fear. These parents are often abusive or abnormally strict. Although individuals with fearful - avoidant attachment style crave intimacy and closeness, they have trouble trusting and depending on others. They do not regulate their emotions well and avoid strong emotional attachments due to fear of rejection or getting hurt.

The reason exploring attachment styles is beneficial when considering single parenthood or family dynamics is because single parent families pose their own unique challenges impacting their parenting style. This, in turn, can affect a child's attachment style in later adult life. For example, a single mother who works multiple shifts may unknowingly and unintentionally neglect her child's emotional needs. From the child's perspective, *'mum is always busy,'* *'mum is always tired'* or *'mum never has time for me'*. With the absence of a father figure combined with emotional neglect from the mother, this can form the child's perception leading to avoidant attachment or NPD in adulthood.

Furthermore, children who grow up without a male figure may have distorted views of masculinity. This 'distortion' can lead to toxic masculinity amongst boys or 'father hunger' amongst females. Father wounds can also manifest itself into dysfunctional relationships. This is because children from fatherless homes do not have the correct 'male guidance' or training to navigate through relationship milestones. As a result, they tend to figure things out through trial and error which can lead to unintentionally breaking someone's heart. In addition, young girls, may observe their mother adopting both masculine and feminine roles (and/or possibly speaking bitterly about their father). This observation can become engrained and normalised within their subconscious - impacting future relationships.

My Story

My family dynamics changed at the age of ten. I grew up in a household with my mother, father, two older sisters and little brother.

Growing up, my father was physically present but emotionally absent. Although I love him unconditionally, at the time, I feared him. He was stern, education focused and God-fearing. The house was always tensed when he was around. At times, it felt as though we could not be children. When we heard the keys rattle (announcing he was home from work) we would quickly switch off the TV, run to get the encyclopedia (he would often assess our understanding), pretend to read the Bible or just start cleaning the house. In short, we had to be seen being productive.

Eventually, my parents announced they were getting a divorce. After the divorce, the home was peaceful. There was no pressure for us to memorise scriptures or read encyclopedias. However, it meant, my mother was forced to work multiple jobs to provide for the family.

How did my family dynamic impact my attachment style?

From an early age, I was able to observe toxicity within the household. From ears dropping my parents' arguments, it was clear there were issues to do with infidelity and a lack of commitment towards the children. I formed an opinion that my father did not love us. It justified his emotional unavailability and unnecessary strictness.

From the outlook, it would have appeared that I developed either an anxious-ambivalent, avoidant, or fearful-avoidant attachment style. However, that was not the case. I never based my value on relationships. In fact, from observing my mother (and other female relatives), all the women were divorced, single or in broken marriages. They each displayed independence, hard work and strength (possibly because they were in 'protective mode'). As a result, I was conditioned (from a young age) to be studious, ambitious, and career driven.

However, after doing further research (and taking the online attachment quiz), I discovered I had a secure attachment style. Although I embrace single life, I also enjoy building long term relationships. In relationships, I am passionate and transparent with my emotions. I can set healthy boundaries and challenge behaviours I do not feel comfortable with.

One of my weaknesses is giving my partner too many chances to get it right. I had to explore the reasons why I was so receptive and forgiving. Surely, it could not be anxious-ambivalent because the thought of being single did not bother me. I concluded that those with secure attachment are intentional with who they date. They rarely jump into relationships, so when they do, it is often for the long haul.

Does this mean the attachment theory is flawed? Not entirely. Although there are some truths to it, it does not consider personal and spiritual growth. It assumes individuals are products of their past. This is accurate if you allow your past to rob you of your future. Therefore, by making peace with your trauma, you reject the label it has on your identity. Too many people fall victims of previous mistakes and use that as a benchmark to make poor decisions; *'I am an alcoholic because I was exposed to alcohol abuse'*. Whilst past situations should be acknowledged, it should not be a crutch. My approach towards life is:

a) Acknowledge how the situation made you feel and heal from it.
b) Reflect on what you have learnt from the situation.
c) Explore ways you can use it to empower yourself and others.

After having an elaborated conversation with a good friend of mine, he disclosed the conflict he endured growing up as the "man" of the house without a father present. He felt obligated to protect his family at an early age. However, the generation gap between him and his sisters made it difficult for him to assert his dominance, presence, and masculinity. I thought that was an interesting finding and decided to dig further into the operation of the male brain (see next page).

LEFT/MASCULINE	RIGHT/FEMININE
differentiating	integrating
individual	collective
external focus	internal focus
part focus	whole focus
results oriented	process oriented
competitive	collaborative
hierarchical structure	circles or swirls
action	planning
doing	being
focus on intent	focus on effect
logic	values
independent	inter-dependent
urgent	patient
analysis	intuition
head	heart
speaking	listening
directing	open
assertive	accommodating
project	respond
conscious	subconscious
structured	random
linear	circule
cause and effect	relationships
linear analysis	systems thinking
bottom-line oriented	stakeholder oriented

Michael Haupt, *Masculine & Feminine, Left- & Right-Brained Thinking Compared*, 2016.

The diagram highlights the differences between the male and female brain. It is almost as though both sexes come from complete opposite worlds with the intention to complement their own (just like daytime and nighttime come together to form an entire day). Naturally, this can lead to an interesting, yet conflicting dynamic between heterosexual couples if polarity is not fostered and understood in a nurturing environment. What do I mean by this?

As mentioned previously, it is important to embrace both masculine and feminine contributions to a relationship without competing or demanding for uniformity (daytime does not compete to be night). Using the example of my friend, it will be absurd to treat and expect him to respond to situations like a woman. An example would be expecting him to know how to communicate his feelings and be expressive. Although vulnerability is something to embrace, for masculine men, it does not always come naturally (due to the wiring of their brain). Despite this, some women get frustrated when men respond to relational conflict logically rather than empathetically. It is important for women to teach men (or masculine energies) the four domains of emotional intelligence (outlined below) to enable them to connect with their feelings and turn intention into action.

1. Self-awareness
2. Self-management
3. Social awareness
4. Relationship management

For instance, when stressed, my friend crawls into his shell and deals with the matter at hand. Once he overcome his hurdles, he communicates it from a place of victory and past tense rather than self-pity. I asked him why he does this. His response was profound. He replied, "*when I am at my weakness point, I cannot let my family know because I am supposed to be their protector. I will feel like a failure if I keep sharing my problems.*' Therefore, by using past tense to articulate his problems, it allows him to subconsciously detach himself from that reality.

To avoid transgressing, it is important to understand the structural differences between both genders in order to fully appreciate and understand their behavior. Using myself as an example, although I naturally respond to events from an emotional place, when communicating with men, I *try* to keep it factual, objective, and logical (whilst expressing the emotional implications it has). This allows for effective communication to take place between both genders.

This stance can be likened to a motorway. If 'person x' was travelling on the left lane whilst 'person y' maintained the right lane, both parties would not be in sync. Therefore, for the purpose of this analogy, couples would need to meet in the middle lane in order to reach their intended destination together. This involves developing mutual understanding, learning, and compromising.

Something to consider: Are behaviours really governed by our biology?

*A*lthough there are scientific evidence suggesting behavior is biological, Sociologists argue gender differences is a result of gender socialization. This starts within the home where parents socialize their children according to their sexes. Men are encouraged to display masculine traits (e.g., hide their feelings) while women are encouraged to be expressive. This attitude is reinforced in secondary socialisation (e.g., education, media etc.) which, in turn, leaks into relationships.

Despite whether gender is biological or societal, it is important to develop mutual understanding between men and women in order to fully comprehend why people behave the way they do. That way, you can eradicate any fears or misconceptions towards members of the opposite sex.

APPLICATION
1) Take an online quiz to find out your attachment style.
2) How does your attachment style affect your current and/or previous relationship?

....
....
....
....
....
....
....
....
....
....
....
....
....
....
....
....
....
....
....
....
....
....
....

4

MODERN DAY CLIMATE

Individuals, today, have become a lot more independent, desensitized, and impatient. This is typically a reactional response to those that may have experienced trauma in previous relationships. When life 'rains,' they respond by either dressing appropriately to avoid getting 'wet', go to extreme measures to avoid the 'rain' or overdress for the 'weather'.

To put into context, relationship breakdowns can be difficult. A healthy way to respond to it is by learning the lessons and assessing areas of development within one's own life. What has this relationship taught me about myself? What issues did my spouse complain about the most? Is this an occurring issue?

Some people, however, lack self-awareness and accountability. As a result, when hurt, they go through extreme measures to avoid experiencing the same pain. For example, they may indulge in promiscuous or unhealthy lifestyles, busy themselves or just become a complete "asshole". It is possible that they use their behaviour as an "umbrella" to shield them from the "rain".

Moreover, it is not uncommon for people to "overdress" for the "weather". In the sense that if they have been hurt or betrayed in the past, they are likely to become guarded, careful, and vigilant throughout the entire relationship. For example, they may display insecurities, need constant reassurance, or be emotionally detached. Dating individuals like this can also be draining and exasperating. Although, I am not advocating to prematurely wear your heart on your sleeves, in my opinion, vulnerability creates room for intimacy. For a relationship to work, both parties need to get "undressed" and "naked" to allow for true intimacy and close connection (figuratively speaking). Indeed, undressing a partner with many layers of clothing, can be time consuming but with patience (an ingredient of Love), it will be worth it!

During a conversation with one of my female students, we discussed the nature of relationships in modern day climate. She described it as "peak". According to her, women today are switched on and becoming worst then men. I asked her to elaborate. To paraphrase, she responded by saying women are becoming emotionally detached and less invested in relationships. They are no longer gullible and have "patterned up". Liberal feminist would argue women's priorities have now changed. Although this can be celebrated as a positive transition, it takes me back to my initial point whereby we are seeing an increase in depolarization. The masculinization of women has led to the feminisation of men (or same sex energy: masculine - masculine) which arguably is unconducive for a healthy relationship.

1) Relationships are heavily influenced by technology and obsessed with vanity:

Gone are the days where people would meet up to truly get to know a person. Nowadays, people hardly meet up. When they do, there is usually an agenda behind it – either to escape boredom or fulfil selfish desires.

Relationships, today, have become far too shallow and short lived. Communication is poor, pictures are glorified, conflict is being had on the phone, relationship problems are broadcasted online, indirect memes are used to express self, and unfollowing has become the new normal.

2) Relationships have become like a fast-food restaurant:

Due to today's "microwave generation", not only are we spoilt for choices (so many options in the menu) but people are quick to get into relationships, quick to break up and quick to move on (or even quick to change their sexuality). This microwave mentality devalues relationships and builds trust issues.

3) Sex had lost its sacredness:

Sex has become far too common and easy to obtain. Most people can detach their emotions from sex and no longer see it as a requirement for a relationship. This, in my opinion, normalises cheating and undermines true intimacy.

SOLUTION BASED ACTIVITY

a) Identify effective ways to deal with conflict in a relationship.

b) Explain the reasons why they are effective.

This can be done independently or with a partner.

5

THE UNIVERSE

The universe has an amazing way of bringing people together. The reason behind it is to fulfil a particular purpose. Relationships are not there to make you happy nor is it there to help you escape loneliness. Rather, the purpose of relationships is to help each other become the-best-version-of-themselves.

The Bible teaches us that *"iron sharpens iron"* (Proverbs 27:17, ESV). This means whoever you build with must be able to support your personal and spiritual growth. It would be impossible for one tool to become sharper without the presence of the other. Left alone, both blades would be dull and useless.

This approach recognises there is someone for everyone. Not everyone has the potential to be your 'iron'. This makes dating life a lot easier. You can filter out who does not add value to your life and date with focus.

Previously, I examined potential partners based on their looks, credentials, and personality. This, however, did nothing for me. I became bored and dissatisfied. My growth was stagnant. I then met someone that inspired me to want to do better. That was when I realised relationships were meaningful when they were purposeful.

The universe aligns you with such people. They are designed to awaken your untapped potential. These types of people fall under the umbrella of 'soul families' – soul mates, twin flames, and even karmic relationships.

Characteristics of a Karmic Relationship

A karmic relationship is a relationship meant to facilitate the lessons we need to learn in this lifetime surrounding love and partnership. Karmic relationships are like teachers. They are temporary. This is because you are coming together to clear karma between each other.

1) There is an instant connection:

The most obvious sign is you feel that you have known the person before. Sometimes, you get a very good feeling about this, but sometimes there is some fear attached.

2) Things feel off early on:

Did you notice a lot of red flags, even in the initial stages of the relationship? Sometimes those triggers are lessons the relationship is trying to teach you, whether that means learning how to heal your own toxic behaviours or how to avoid such unhealthy dynamics in the future.

3) They do not last:

Because karmic relationships can often become unhealthy, it's important to recognize that the point is not to stay in that toxic dynamic. The point is to learn from what's not working, and to leave. Eventually, when you're ready and have learned the lessons, you're meant to learn, you will both move on.

Characteristics of a Twin Flame

7 win flames are the same soul shared between two physical beings. For this reason, you can only have one twin flame (not everyone has one). They are divided between masculine and feminine energies and constantly yearn for each other.

1) Twin flames are mirrors, not Twins:

Twin flame love is about spiritual growth. Their relationship is tumultuous (off and on). They shine a light on insecurities and fears which causes separation periods - where both parties are forced to work on themselves.

2) Similarities in life experiences and a lot of uncanny alignments:

Twin flames usually have similar moral compass, experiences, and traumas. They also share mutual interests or reciprocal traits, such as hobbies, talents, passion, and personalities.

3) Instant connection:

When twin flames first meet, there is an intense attraction, emotional connection, longing, and recognition. They feel familiar and share an undeniable bond which is predestined.

Characteristics of a Soulmate

U nlike twin flames, you can have many soulmates. Soul mates are two separate souls that are linked. They are contracted to have relationships within this physical incarnation. Before coming into plane, we chose to learn specific lessons from specific people.

1) The timing is right:

You are both on the same page, commitment-wise, and you're a good fit in other areas.

2) You can pick up on their emotions easily:

They call it couples' intuition: You can read your partner without them even saying a word.

3) They add value to your life:

According to popular thought, soulmates "complete" you, but you're complete just the way you are. Instead, the right person enhances your life.

6

THE STAR

Before entering the 'seasons of a relationship', it is important to undergo self-assessment. As holistic beings, we are the *star* of the universe. Evolution and science confirm this. They remind us that humans are unusual, complex, and intelligent beings. We are made up of physical, intellectual, emotional, social, and spiritual components. Therefore, our singleness is a period where we focus on each component and uproot any troublesome weeds of past wounds that can impact our holistic development.

Yet, society frowns on being single. Negative connotations are used to frame singledom. It is seen as a lonely and hopefully temporary state. The notion that someone might want to be on their own, perhaps for a long while, terrifies the world. Advertisers patronise, overcharge, and demean anyone who has the impudence to venture on their own - by showing tantalising images of happy couples on 'baecations'.

This is not a healthy attitude to have towards singlehood. It places pressure on individuals to couple up – leading to emotional desperation. When someone is starving, they eat anything – even if it kills them. Sadly, some people adopt this approach towards dating. They settle for anyone. The urgency to update social media about their relationship status is linked to their self-worth. However, it is important to note that being alone is not synonyms to rejection. It is an indicator that you have considered the available options and — with wisdom — have done some rejecting yourself.

As a selective individual, I am particular with who I call my life partner. Your heart alone does not cut it. Why? Because I have hustled in this life independently. I am comfortable with myself and enjoy my own company. As a result, I look for (and deserve) someone who can add value and contribute to my life - not just keep me company. Expectations matter.

In summary, being at ease with your singleness is the needed, secure platform to make a sane and wise choice about who to create joint life with. There are practical steps you can take to utilise your singleness. Remember, you are the *star* in someone's universe!

ENHANCING YOUR PHYSICAL
DEVELOPMENT DURING SINGLENESS

*E*nhancing your physical development is also classified as 'body love'. Although some may deem this form of love as vain and superficial, it is important to take pride in the way we look, and, of course, our health. Not only does it improve self-image, but it encourages body confidence.

1. You are what you eat:

The notion that 'you are what you eat' stems from the idea that to be fit and healthy, you must pay attention to the food you consume.

During your singleness, it is recommended you learn to cook a range of healthy dishes. Not only would it be appreciated by your future partner (and children), but it is a known fact that healthy eating boosts energy levels and appearance.

2. Hit the gym:

Exercising also has many health benefits. Not only does it keep your body in shape, but it increases the production of endorphins, improves sexual health and your overall skin appearance.

During your singleness, practice moving around. Dancing and yoga are great ways to develop sexual confidence, overcome body shyness and improve flexibility.

3. Find beauty within you and define it:

Look in the mirror and re-evaluate your appearance. Create your own beauty standards and embrace it. What are you happy with and what areas require improvement? If you would like to lose or gain weight, stop talking about it and start creating SMART targets. This helps keep you focused, accountable and ensures you meet your body goal.

4. Rest:

We live in a society where everyone wants to appear busy and productive. However, part of being productive requires resting and slowing down. That way, you do not drain your body or look like a tired mess!

SELF- REFLECTION

- **How can I improve my diet?**

  ....

- **What are my body goals?**

  ....

- **What do I like about my appearance?**

  ....

- **If my body could talk, what would it tell me?**

  ....

ENHANCING YOUR INTELLECTUAL DEVELOPMENT DURING SINGLENESS

7 eeding your mind during your singleness is equally important. When we are in alignment with loving the mind, we focus on our mental strengths, we celebrate our personal intelligence, accomplishments and challenge ourselves to new heights. Undoubtedly, this has many benefits in relationships. It makes you an interesting person, self-assured and high value.

1. Discover your purpose and work towards it:

I am a firm believer that God has given everyone an assignment. It is up to you to unravel your calling and work towards it. When you keep yourself busy, you find little time to dwell on your singleness.

2. Avoid mind numbing activities (e.g., binge-watching pointless TV shows):

Once you discover your purpose, you would realise time is precious. You do not have time to engage in pointless activities or enter meaningless relationships.

3. You are what you hear:

Faith comes from hearing. What are you listening to? Is it edifying you?

4. Stimulate the mind:

Like the muscle, we must 'train' the mind to build mental strength. One of the best ways to do this is through learning. Learning can be as simple as reading books or having thought provoking conversations with people.

5. Review your mental health:

You are what you think. Negative self-perception should not be overlooked. If you think poorly of yourself, guess what? It will be manifested into self-doubt, low self-esteem and potentially people pleasing. This can make you an easy target to abusive relationships.

SELF – REFLECTION

- **What is my life purpose?**

....

- **What are my talents?**

....

- **What are my strengths and weakness?**

....

- **What skills do I want to develop? How?**

....

- **What am I most proud of?**

....

ENHANCING YOUR EMOTIONAL DEVELOPMENT DURING SINGLENESS

Singlehood is an opportunity to pay attention to your emotions and how you feel about yourself. Once we become our own best friends, we become content with our presence. This helps reduce loneliness and dependency on others. Unsurprisingly, people treat you based on how you treat yourself. If you suffer from insecurities, anger issues, narcissistic traits, poor attachment styles, or you are simply healing from a previous breakup, sort it out! No one wants to babysit an emotionally unstable person. Nor is it fair to make someone else life difficult because of your unresolved trauma.

Your singleness is also an opportunity to do what makes you happy. The happier we are on our own, the more radiant we become. We can exercise the correct degree of caution when finding a companion and walk away from 'deals' that does not serve us. Thus, the bedrock of true love is happy singledom.

1. Discover your love language:

Do not wait for someone to cater to your needs. Do it yourself. That way, you are not easily impressed by mere effort. Nor do you give "co-dependency" vibes.

2. Find out what your triggers are:

Find out what your triggers are, analyse why they are triggers and heal from it. Previously, one of my triggers was being ignored. This could be as simple as someone not responding to an email or taking too long to text back. I found it incredibly rude and took it personally.

After doing a deep dive into my "trigger," I realised it stemmed from being ignored in my previous "relationship". The guy I was dating would often use the silent treatment as a form of punishment. Afterwards, he would blame me for his actions. Consequently, I associated being ignored to doing something wrong.

3. Find ways to manage your emotions:

Are you emotionally impulsive? Do you react impulsively when experiencing a heightened situation? If that is the case, find better ways to manage your emotions during your singleness. This could be via exercising, journaling, or venting to close family and friends.

If you are like me, you may also be innately expressive. Meaning, you wear your heart on your sleeves. Although this can be a good thing, bleeding next to sharks makes you vulnerable to attacks. Thus, your singleness is a time to exercise discipline and practice "mouth control". Not everyone needs to have access to your heart, thoughts, or emotions.

SELF- REFLECTION

- **What are my insecurities?**

  ....

- **What is my love language?**

  ....

- **What do I like about myself?**

  ....

- **What are my attachment and conflict styles?**

  ....

- **Would I marry someone like me?**

  ....

ENHANCING YOUR SOCIAL DEVELOPMENT DURING SINGLENESS

*A*ccording to Maslow, individuals crave a sense of community and belonging. Your singleness is an opportunity to build, enjoy and strengthen friendships. Meaningful friendships come in handy when entering a relationship or going through relationship seasons. Your friends become your "eyes" when you have rose tinted glasses on. They become your "shoulder" when you need a shoulder to cry on. They become your "brain" when you are just not thinking properly. In short, investing in quality friendships is key to improving your holistic development.

1. Plan trips with friends:

Whilst you are single, book vacations with your friends. This not only solidifies your interaction but makes single life enjoyable (you do not need to seek permission from anyone, and you can let your hair down without feeling guilty).

2. Join classes and workshops:

Build friendships with like-minded people. Joining classes enables you to interact with individuals that share similar interest as yourself.

3. Go on dates:

You have no ties to anyone so enjoy going on dates. The more dates you go on, the more choices you have. Just make sure you date with integrity!

4. Spend time with family and friends:

Spend quality time with family and friends. Remember, when you get into a relationship, that time will be divided so take advantage of it!

5. Attend networking events:

You will be amazed by the opportunities you get from just networking. You may not always end up as business partners, but it can be a start to a fruitful relationship.

SELF – REFLECTION

- **How can I meet like-minded people?**

  ....

- **How can I build closer bonds with my family and friends?**

  ....

- **How would my friends describe me?**

  ....

- **Am I fun to be around with?**

  ....

ENHANCING YOUR SPIRITUAL DEVELOPMENT DURING SINGLENESS

*7*his is the deepest aspect of self-love. Loving your spirit might involve a spiritual or religious practice. When we get in touch with our own definition of a higher power (or even purpose), we take care of our deep self. This can be done through prayer, study, meditation, or whatever practice feels natural to you. For some, this might be as simple as sitting outdoors and enjoying nature.

1. Be still:

Many tend to get caught up in the hustle and bustle of the material world but feel empty inside. Be still and appreciate the wonderful things God has done for you. Be still and know that God has good things in store for you. Be still and know that you serve a good God. Be still and know that it's going to be OK.

2. Revisit your values, beliefs, and principles:

Imagine entering a relationship without any values, belief systems or non-negotiables. How do you think that would work out for you? Once you have strong belief systems and core values, you are able set healthy and unapologetic boundaries. You become a positive influence towards those around you and you ooze confidence.

3. Forge a closer relationship with God:

Do not advertise your faith like a poster when there is little substance. Use this time to get in touch with your Creator.

4. Pray and meditate:

God promises to give you your heart desires. He gave us key principles to follow. Write your visions down, make it clear and pray about it. Simple.

SELF – REFLECTION

- **What are my values and core beliefs?**

  ....

- **What are my prayer points?**

  ....

- **What *weeds* does God need to uproot to make me a high value person?**

  ....

- **What makes me unique?**

  ....

After doing a holistic self-assessment, you would understand why your singleness is an important phrase in your life. It is the groundwork to make you a well-rounded and high value individual which will enrich your future relationships.

According to Syrtash, "the best relationships occur when you have a good understanding of your needs, wants and values."

7

THE SEASONS

Just like the weather, relationships also go through several seasons - spring, summer, autumn, and winter. Each season has temperatures which prompts changes. They may not always occur in systematic order, but they are undeniable. For example, the British weather is known to experience all four seasons within a particular month. During summer, there may be episodes of rain and cold breeze. In fact, throughout the summer of 2021, Britain experienced floods, thunderstorms, and extreme heat warnings. According to geographers, the changeable weather was "down to the jet stream."

To put into context, external factors can influence temperatures within a relationship. For example, during *spring* (dating stage), couples may experience *drizzle* or *rain*. This can symbolise minor conflict. It is up to both parties to tackle the *rain* rather than complaining about the *weather*.

Let us put this into perspective. If you had to go to work but it was raining, would you stay home and complain about the weather or pick up an umbrella and fight through the rain? Most people would opt for the latter. This is because they see value in their job. It pays the bills and offers job-satisfaction. If, however, you decided to stay home and shy away from the rain, this would lead to you potentially losing your job. You would be deemed 'unreliable.'

The same applies to relationships. Despite the differing temperatures, individuals must remain faithful to each other and God's Word. The Word is the 'umbrella' that helps you weather the storm. Thus, in terms of adversary, couples must remain patient and kind. Sadly, we live in a generation where people are too proud and discontent. They allow their ego and pride to interfere with their decision-making when exposed to a little *drizzle*.

The next few chapters of the book identifies the four seasons in a relationship. It guides couples on how to 'dress for the weather' to ensure momentum. Before exploring each phase, it is worth noting that all couples will experience different seasons at some point in their relationship. This is necessary to strengthen and build connection. It makes relationships meaningful and worthwhile.

As you read this book, you would begin to realise that although the *summer* period is often exciting, it has potential of becoming dull, static, and monotonous if emotions are not challenged. It is essential that couples are kept on their toes to avoid complacency because the sad reality is we "often take for granted the very thing that deserves our gratitude." In short, during *summer*, we may become familiarised with the *heat*, that we begin to devalue its scarcity. Only, until we experience *winter*, do we appreciate the joys of *summer*.

Does this mean *winter* is healthy for a functioning relationship? To some degree, yes. Although, some people may fear the cold, *winter* is an inevitable part of a relationship. It is what test the relationship and holds couples together. Couples can reflect on how to climatise to the weather and apply effective strategies.

It is imperative that couples remember relationship takes hard work, maturity, resilience, commitment, and a lot of forgiveness. The book is aimed to help couples adapt to each season without giving up.

8

SPRING (THE DATING STAGE)

Spring is the first season of any relationship and is usually the happiest. It is often associated with a time of rebirth, renewal, and awakening. Trees blossom during these period and early flowers push through the earth. From a Christian angle, it is also a period of resurrection (when Jesus rose from the dead - three days after being executed and crucified). Christians around the world celebrate this moment with great triumphant and joy as it is a reminder that they are reborn and made new.

How can this be applied to relationships? As spring suggest 'new beginnings', – it can also be the start of new relationships. Individuals may have experienced their personal 'crucifixion' in previous relationship which left them battered and bruised. Some may argue their 'crucifixion' was a necessary part of their growth. There is something miraculous about walking through the shadows of death knowing that 'goodness and mercy will follow you' (Psalms 23:6). In this context, although your past may have seemed messy, your future can still look spotless (if you tidy it up).

Thus, *spring* is the time when you pick up the bricks that life threw at you and start building towers. You reflect on previous mistakes, learn the lessons, and make necessary adjustments to ensure your new and profound relationship does not resemble your past. You may undergo drastic changes to your mind-set, appearance, or habits. There has been a renewal of self. This is an exciting period for you as the future begins to look promising.

However, before entering a relationship, it is important to first have a healthy relationship with yourself (as mentioned previously). Spring clean your mess before allowing anyone else into your home. That way, you will not contaminate them with your germs and your reputation remains protected.

In other words, we all have mental, emotional, spiritual, and relational scars. If left unattended, these scars can reappear and choke potential relationships. It is important to uproot any troublesome weeds of past wounds during our singleness to ensure our new relationship remains healthy.

Bruce Tuckman (1965) developed a team development model which examines the five stages a team goes through to become successful. This model can be applied to relationships.

1) **Forming:** when the team first come together.

2) **Storming:** when conflict arises within the team.

3) **Norming:** when the team establish ground rules on how to work effectively.

4) **Performing:** when the team is stable. There is a sense of focus and purpose.

5) **Adjourning:** when the goals of the team have been accomplished.

As you can see from the diagram, relationships go through a series of ups and downs. The initial stage is the *forming* stage which occurs during *spring* (dating stage) and *summer* (honeymoon period). In both seasons, emotions are high. There are a lot of happiness, romance, and excitement. This is the time when couples get to know each other. According to

Tuckman, individuals, during this phase, avoid conflict and 'play nice'. Arguably, women tend to fall quickly during this stage. They are captivated by men's words and men are obsessed with the female's aesthetics.

FIVE WAYS TO 'DRESS' FOR SPRING
(DATING SEASON)

*I*t is important to nurture your flowers during spring so that they can grow and blossom in summer. In the context of relationship, the dating stage also requires nurturing. It needs to be watered with love, care, and attention. This helps cement the relationship.

1) Ask questions to gauge compatibility and build emotional intimacy:

Research by psychologists Arthur Aron, and his wife, Elaine Aron (1990s) developed the idea that individuals can build emotional closeness by asking a series of questions. This study has been used in marriage counselling to accelerate the creation of closeness and intimacy. Asking questions not only allows for bonding but enables both parties to determine whether they are compatible.

2) Set boundaries:

Setting boundaries and voicing expectations is healthy and necessary in the beginning of a relationship. It helps keep both parties safe and reduces conflict. For example, you may wish to set physical boundaries (this

71

refers to body, privacy and/or personal space), sexual boundaries (refers to expectations around physical intimacy) or intellectual boundaries (in references to values and beliefs).

3) Create a bucket list of what you would like to achieve:

Having a bucket list not only creates excitement in a relationship but ensures your relationship is productive, challenging, and focused. What holidays should we go on this year? What books should we read together? What skills should we develop?

4) Go on dates:

Going on dates is another fun way to bond and create memories. It allows you to observe your potential partner in different settings – (which can also help determine whether they are a suitable candidate).

5) Pray:

Do not be led by your emotions. Rather, pray this prayer: "Thank you for 'person x'. Your Word says you only have good things in store for me. If this is the person you have ordained for me to be with, may Your will be done. Amen."

FIVE WAYS TO PROTECT YOURSELF DURING SPRING

S ince this is a very shallow stage in your relationship, it is easy to be blinded by infatuation. Therefore, to guard your heart, you must remain vigilant, cautious, and observant.

1) Do your research:

Some questions can only be answered through your own private investigation. Social media and the internet make it easier to dig out a person's history.

In addition, the Claire's Law (2014) allow individuals to make enquiries about their potential interest. If police checks show a potential partner has a record of abusive behaviour, or information to indicate that you may be at risk, the police will consider sharing this information with you. The scheme aims to help individuals make informed decisions when entering or continuing a relationship.

You may feel intrusive doing this, but it is better to safeguard yourself from potential abuse. Think about it like this, if an employer can research a potential employee, why can't you research a potential partner?

2) Action speaks louder than words:

'Don't let someone's words blind you from their behaviour' Steve Maraobi. Too often, people will sell you dreams. Eventually, you would be able to monitor gaps in their behaviour. Pay attention to that. Not all words are spoken.

3) Listen to your intuition:

If something feels off, it usually is. Do not let anyone tell you, you are overthinking, 'mad' or paranoid. If you have a nagging feeling that something isn't right, rather than pocketing your intuition, confront the person and observe their reaction. Alternatively, pray about it or make a silent decision and leave.

4) Observe patterns and behaviours:

After speaking to a friend and ex colleague, Devon Waite, he advised that it is important to 'identify a person's bad trait and determine whether you can live with it. If you cannot, there is no point in pursuing a relationship'. This is true because the red flags you observe at the beginning are usually the reasons you end up leaving.

5) Pray:

Pray this prayer: 'Thank you for giving me the spirit of discernment, wisdom, and knowledge so that I can date with caution. I ask that you continue to open my eyes and expose the character of 'person x'. If this person is not from you, I pray that you remove them from my life. Amen'.

Relationship Inventory

*A*fter deciding to go ahead with a relationship, a conversation needs to be had – (usually from the masculine energy). A good friend of mine shared that every three months, she, and her husband would have a 'relationship inventory' where they would each communicate what is going well in the relationship and areas of development.

This ritual is worth practicing even at the conception stages of a relationship. This normalises open communication and allows for transparency in a safe environment.

In addition, it is beneficial to have a 'relationship inventory' before approaching the next transition of the relationship as it eliminates confusion and prevents being in a situationship or textationship (the terms alone are confusing).

In practical sense, the 'relationship inventory' involves both parties deciding whether to take a leap of faith and become exclusive. Some people may question how long *spring* should last. When is the right time to take that leap of faith? How do I know if I am ready to commit myself to this person? Although these questions are relative to the individuals involved, I do not think *spring* should prolong. If after 'dressing appropriately for the weather' and taking the necessary precautions, you still feel a sense of compatibility – then it may be worth taking that risk. Remember, relationships are where we learn the most about ourselves. It is not a life-sentence. It does not have to last forever. If it does not work out, it means the universe is preparing you for someone better!

With that being said, it is important to be decisive and avoid prolonging the dating stage. This is because as time progresses, both parties naturally go through Tuckman's group model - the 'storming' stage. This is when conflict arises (discussed in the next chapter). When conflict arises prematurely before a relationship begins, it is easy for both parties to give up and see it as a sign of incompatibility. However, that is not the case. Conflict is an inevitable part of *any* relationship. It exposes elements of an individual's character (which they tend to conceal in the beginning). Moreover, it allows both parties to observe how each deal with disagreement, what triggers them and what values they uphold. From experience, conflict is best had in a committed relationship rather than during 'spring' (dating stage).

Why do I say this? Having relationship problems with someone you are not in a relationship with is confusing and a waste of time. When mentoring young girls, I encourage them to avoid being emotionally invested during the dating stage. In practice, this can be difficult as women are emotional by nature. They are not coached to have an emotional backbone. Rather, they think with their hearts and act on their feelings.

However, unless you enjoy being sad, you should avoid giving men access to your heart. It is delicate and should be reserved for your husband only. Albert Einstein once said, *'if you want to live a happy life, tie it to a goal, not to people or things.'* The reason behind it is self-explanatory. However, the point made is people can hurt you. So, to limit the amount of people that hurt you, you must be selective with who you let inside your world. This means; stop arguing, sending long paragraphs, or trying to make 'sense' of a situation with someone you are not committed to. If a guy likes you, he will pursue you. If he doesn't pursue you, he doesn't like you. Period.

One way to determine whether someone is genuine or whether it is worth transitioning to the next stage, is by undertaking the Prince Charming test. This test was formulated by Kara King in her book *'The Power of the Pussy'*. The test recognises that love is based on actions not speech! Some men are far too talkative. They talk the good game, but their actions are fruitless.

To perform this test, you must put yourself in a position of need (damsel in distress) and observe whether your potential partner would run to your rescue.

My Story

Although things did not work out with my previous partner, I cannot ignore the number of times he would come to my rescue (even after we broke up). He would often inconvenience himself to make sure I and my family were comfortable.

For example:

- *He would sort out anything concerning my car.*
- *He would travel long distance (irrespective of the time) whenever I (or my family) needed him.*
- *He would babysit my niece and nephew so that me and their mum could go out.*

One thing that stood out for me was when he travelled from South London to the outskirts of London (in the middle of the night) to pick me up from an event. Although he was annoyed throughout the entire journey, his actions confirmed his commitment.

Although I did not intend to perform The Prince Charming test on him, it goes to show, a man that likes a woman, would jump through hoops to help her.

Paradoxically, I was later faced with an individual who claimed to like me. When the time arose, I performed The Prince Charming test on him (by putting myself in a vulnerable position and observing his reaction). He failed each time.

For example:

- *I asked him to phone me because I was in perceived danger. He responded by saying he was in the cinema.*

- *I asked him to phone me so that I could 'offload'. He responded by saying he was busy, and I should phone my friend.*

Although these examples now seem laughable, at the time, I was hurt and confused. Upon reflection, it is a quick and efficient way to filter out timewasters. It gives you a snapshot of how invested an individual is towards you. Despite these clear red flags, I was blinded by his charm. I believed his words and excused his actions. He would often give me the false impression that he felt strongly for me and would one day commit. I foolishly waited trusting the 'connection' we shared combined with his words. Fast forward, I discovered he was a womanizer and a persuasive, pathological liar!

In Summary:

- Be cautious during the dating stage – avoid being too invested.

- Observe their actions – not just their words.

- Do your research, pray, and put your potential partner to test before transitioning to the next stage.

- Avoid prolonging the dating stage.

- Avoid having relationship problems with someone you are not in a relationship with.

9

SUMMER (THE HONEYMOON PERIOD)

Like *spring, summer* is also associated with happy moments. Couples experience love in its most immature form – infatuation. This is a foolish type of love where we only see our partner with rose tinted glasses. During this period, couples still undergo the *forming* stage. They do not entirely know each other. Their focus is on maintaining peace and building bonds. As a result, they tend to overlook red flags; ignore, bear, or forgive each other's mistakes and bad habits. Issues are commonly swept under the carpet and arguments are avoided.

During this stage, both individuals may take a leap of faith and become exclusive. Again, emotions are high. Everything seems carefree and fun. Some people see this period as the most exciting part of their relationship and aim to prolong it. This is because the honeymoon period is when the brain releases a cocktail of chemicals (oxytocin, phenylethylamine, serotonin, and dopamine) designed to make the heart thump. It can be likened to an addictive drug – causing a temporary high. The 'moon' aspect of the term signifies the 'honey' phase is short lived and temporary (just like a drug).

It is no surprise that couples aim to maintain the *summer* season in their relationship. To do so, it is imperative they develop holistic intimacy. This requires building a physical, mental, emotional, experimental, and spiritual connection with each other.

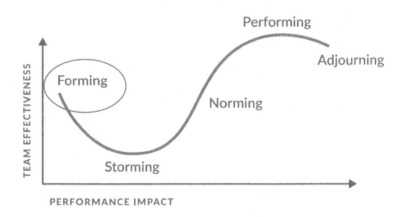

FIVE WAYS TO 'DRESS' FOR SUMMER
(HONEYMOON SEASON)

1) Develop physical intimacy:

Physical intimacy is about touch and closeness between bodies. In romantic relationships, it involves serving each other with your body. For example, you may wish to express physical affection by holding hands, cuddling, kissing, massaging, or performing tantrism (a slow and meditative form of intimacy involving the sensations of the body).

2) Mental stimulation:

Find out what stimulates your partner mentally. For example, as a creative individual, I gravitate towards conversations that allows me think creatively and artistically. I also enjoy having discussions about topical issues (inspired by books, documentaries and/or podcast). This form of intellectual intimacy enables couples to expand each other's minds and challenge perspectives.

3) Prioritising emotional intimacy:

This is were having regular 'relationship inventory' is beneficial (as discussed in page 76). Sharing thoughts

*and feelings creates space for transparency. Both
parties can express their emotions freely and openly
without judgement. Couples that prioritises emotional
intimacy usually end up having healthier relationships.*

4) Spend quality time:

*Be intentional with your dates. Plan something exciting
and regularly. This allows you to give birth to
wonderful memories and generate closeness. An
example of experiential intimacy can involve booking
trips, doing activities (e.g., gym), cooking a new recipe,
working on a project, or starting a new hobby together.*

5) Develop your spiritual life together:

*This can involve meditating, praying, practicing
mindfulness, connecting with nature, or attending
relationship seminars. Again, it is important to invite
God throughout your relationship journey – not just
when things are rocky!*

FIVE WAYS TO 'PROTECT' YOURSELF DURING SUMMER

*A*s mentioned previously, the honeymoon period is like a drug. It is easy to become delusional and see our partner in their purest form. The biggest scam is people during this stage tend to be unintentionally dishonest. They conceal their dark side and present their bright side.

Individuals may also develop an unhealthy obsession with each other and demonstrate clingy behaviours. This can quickly lead to boredom or the other person feeling overwhelmed.

1) Manage expectations:

Do not run before you can crawl. In this case, take things slowly. Do not rush into anything hastily. For example, avoid moving into each other's apartments or setting up joint accounts. Remember, you are still getting to know each other. So, avoid fast tracking the curriculum before studying the course (figuratively speaking).

2) Avoid documenting everything on social media:

Not everyone needs to know your business. You do not need to declare to the world how 'person x' makes you feel or every pivotal moment of your relationship. Some things need to be kept confidential for the health of your relationship.

3) Introduce them to close family and friends:

It is easy to have a bias view of your person. Therefore, it may be worth introducing them to close family members or friends to gauge an objective account. Parents are usually a good judge of character. Not only do they have good intentions for you, but they share life experience which enables them to discern a person's toxic trait.

4) Create space:

It is important to have your own hobbies and interest outside the relationship. Avoid prioritising your relationship to the point that you lose your identity. By creating space, you allow yourself to recharge and process your thoughts. This is essential to avoid feeling suffocated and trapped in the early stages of your relationship. You may decide to spend 40% of your time with your partner and the remaining 60% on self.

5) Pray:

Pray this prayer: 'Thank you for bringing 'person x' in my life. I pray that you continue to strengthen our friendship and draw us closer to you. Help us to bring out the best in each other' Amen.

Relationship Inventory

*D*uring the honeymoon period, it is important to set time aside to discuss how the relationship is going. Feel free to highlight what is going well. What has your partner done that made you feel loved, safe, and heard? By acknowledging these areas, your partner is bound to feel appreciated.

You may wish to go the extra mile and reward those positive behaviours. This strategy is known as 'positive reinforcement' – a term developed by B. F. Skinner during the 1930s and 1940s. He argued that an action is strengthened by rewards, leading to repetition of the desired behaviour.

This means if your partner has demonstrated a good deed, it is important to celebrate their effort by rewarding them based on their love language - a concept created by marriage counsellor, Gary Chapman, 1992 (see next page).

Love Language	Description	Example of rewards
Words of affirmation	People with this love language place high value on verbal expression	Explain in detail how their behaviour made you feel. Compliment.
Acts of service	People with this love language place high value on actions	Do small acts that makes them feel appreciated. Cook dinner / iron clothes. Wash their car.
Receiving gifts	People with this love language place high value on tangible items	Buy a thoughtful gift. Send flowers (even if it isn't a special occasion). Buy their favorite snack.
Quality time	People with this love language place high value on the time you spend together	Plan a date. Play a board game. Take a mini road trip.
Physical touch	People with this love language place high value on receiving affection through touch and physical closeness.	Give them a massage. Kiss them passionately. Cuddle while you're talking.

However, no matter how compatible you are, it is common for couples to experience a little 'drizzle' during *summer*. This can symbolise a misunderstanding or poor communication. When this happens, it is important to tackle the issue immediately.

From experience, the *summer* season needs to be nurtured with a lot of love, attention, and care. This ensures the person you are involved with does not feel neglected. When neglect occurs, it is easy for the other person to feel insecure and ignored. They may fight for your attention by sparking pointless arguments which can lead to the premature death of your relationship.

The remedy for this is to be attentive to each other's needs and constantly dress for the weather.

My Story

Relationship suicide can occur when both parties fail to develop holistic intimacy. In my previous situation with someone, communication was poor and quality time lacked. When these fundamental components are missing, it allows assumptions to be made, trust issues to be magnified, and guards to be up. This is damaging in the early stages of a relationship as it is not being watered with love, care, and attention. The foundations are weak.

In Summary:

- Develop your bond by applying holistic intimacy.

- Find innovative ways to cater to each other's love language.

- Remember, you are still under the 'honeymoon drug', so take caution!

- Ask yourself this question, 'does their action confirm their words?'

- Have a life outside the relationship. Do not let the relationship become your identity.

10

AUTUMN (THE CONFLICTUAL STAGE)

Autumn is a season where we see mixed temperatures. At this stage, you begin to observe faults in your partner. This is the storming stage in Tuckman's model where arguments arise. According to Tuckman, people's true colours are revealed. Efforts may decline and behaviours may change. Most people during this stage give up as they experience a change in weather. They no longer feel the butterflies they once had and view it as a sign that the love has gone. As a result, individuals may withdraw, have wandering eyes, or decide to go their separate paths.

This is not a time to panic, so relax! It simply means your relationship has transitioned to the *autumn* stage of your relationship. If built on solid grounds, you will be able to weather the storm (hence why nurturing *spring* and *summer* is essential). This is because you both recognise the value of your relationship. By working collaboratively, you begin to tackle the issue as a team rather than in solitude.

As you can see from the diagram above, emotions are at its lowest. This is because although you may have liked each other, you did not fully know or trust one other. Trust is the superglue of relationships. It can take a long time to build. We must, therefore, be ruthless with the smallest weed of mistrust that pops up in our relationship soil.

Unsurprisingly, once tension or distrust arises, guards

rise. Individuals may respond by withdrawing or separating – rather than dealing with the root cause. Depending on which party became emotionally invested, feelings are likely to get hurt as the other person becomes emotionally distant. You may find yourself in a cat and mouse situation where you begin chasing for their attention and affection. Don't do this! If love is not reciprocated, it can be self-destructive.

Sadly, it is common for couples to give up during the 'storming' stage. This is because they have a short-sighted lens when it comes to viewing their relationship. They cannot see the bigger picture. Consequently, some individuals may begin to explore their options. They are under the false pretence that the grass is greener on the other side.

However, just like spring has hot and cool temperatures - so do relationships. Individuals may decide to reconcile having realised their relationship is worth fighting for (this may take a couple of days, weeks or even months). Once both parties agree to reconcile, changes need to be made. If not, they run the risk of having the same arguments but in different formats. This can lead to an on-again, off-again relationship (which is emotionally irresponsible, distressing, and embarrassing).

Once committed, both partners must agree to climatise to the weather irrespective of the storm (unless it is a toxic situation). This means they both anticipate there would be rain, thunder, lightning, sunshine and even snow! Yet, they are equally prepared to dress according to the weather. For this reason, it is important to select a high value partner who has the emotional maturity to undergo climate change with you.

After the 'storming' stage, Tuckman hypothesised individuals will naturally progress to the 'norming' phase of the relationship. In this stage, clear ground rules are established, and couples work collaboratively. As temperatures begin to get warmer, both parties realise they are a team. They resolve differences and aim to work harmoniously by applying effective communication.

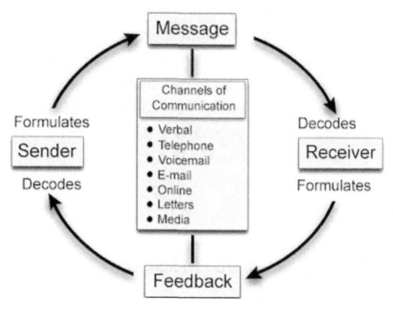

Linear Communication Model, 2014

Michael Argle, a British psychologist, developed a model called 'the communication cycle' (see diagram above). The model is used to demonstrate effective communication in intimate settings. According to Argyle, communication is a learnt process. It requires mastery. He compared it to driving a car. Both needs constant evaluating, reviewing, and adjusting. Attentiveness to road conditions is imperative to avoid accidents. Similarly, attentiveness to verbal and nonverbal cues is imperative to avoid misinterpretations.

Today, people communicate using a range of different

channels, such as text, phone calls, social media or in person. However, when discussing a serious concern in your relationship, it is best to communicate in person. This helps avoid misunderstanding.

APPLYING THE 'COMMUNICATION CYCLE' IN RELATIONSHIPS

Step 1 - An idea occurs:

The sender has an idea of what they would like to communicate to the receiver.

For example, Mary may wish to communicate her feelings to Tom. However, to ensure effective communication takes place, Mary must be clear in her thoughts. This prevents waffling.

Step 2 – Message Encoded:

This is the mental process where the sender considers the most suitable way to translate the information using appropriate channels of communication.

For example, Mary may decide to speak in person rather than disclosing her feelings via text or social media.

Step 3 - Message Sent:

This is when the sender dispatches the message to the

receiver.

For example, Mary will share her feelings with Tom. Whilst doing so, she will consider her tone of voice and body language.

Step 4 – Message Delivered:

This is when the message gets delivered to the receiver.

For example, Tom would hear the points made by Mary. To ensure this is done successfully, it is important there are no barriers that would hinder effective communication from taking place (e.g., external noise).

Step 5 – Message Decoded:

This is the stage where the receiver interprets the message sent by the sender.

The process allows Tom to clarify what has been said by asking questions to ensure comprehension and avoid misinterpretation.

Step 6 – Message Understood:

This is the final stage of the communication cycle where the receiver demonstrates understanding by formulating a response. With this step, the receiver becomes the sender, and applies the same clarity of thought in their feedback.

Once you both know how to communicate effectively, the next step is to discover your conflict style. Of course, conflict in any setting can be uncomfortable. It is even more distressing having disputes with someone you love. However, once you know how to manage conflict, it can lead to healthier relationships. In fact, walking towards conflict is a chance to deepen relationships. It is not the adversary of connection.

Collaborating Style

This is a combination of being assertive and cooperative. Couples that collaborate attempt to work together to identify a solution that satisfies each other.

This style of conflict is suitable when you value both the relationship and are keen to reach an outcome to the solution.

Competing Style

This type of conflict has a firm stance. Individuals with this conflict style are assertive and uncooperative. They refuse to listen to their partner's perspective and will continue to reject their ideas until they get their way.

In other words, they are more interested in getting their voices heard. This communicates a lack of care, empathy or understanding which can damage a relationship.

Avoiding Style

Those with avoiding style completely evades the conflict. They tend to be unassertive and uncooperative. Individuals with this conflict style will sidestep or withdraw from an issue.

They do not care enough about the outcome and take a laidback approach to the matter. This style is appropriate when the conflict is trivial and not worth arguing about.

Accommodating Style

People with this type of conflict style are more interested in satisfying the person rather than the outcome. They are happy to forsake their own needs or desires in exchange for their partner. In short, they self-sacrifice their needs to maintain peace.

Compromising Style

A compromising style attempts to find a solution which pleases both parties. Their aim is to reach a middle ground.

The most appropriate conflict style depends on the nature of the disagreement. Sometimes, it is best to avoid investing too much time and energy on an issue if it is petty. On the flip side, this can communicate to your spouse a lack of urgency to fix it - causing further frustration.

REFLECTION

a. What is your conflict style?
b. Is it compatible with your partner's? If not, how can you ensure conflict compatibility?
c. Think about a time you had a disagreement with your partner, did you demonstrate effective communication? If so, how? If not, why not?

APPLICATION

Pick an issue you would like to discuss with your partner. Consider an effective conflict management style to use whilst applying the communication cycle. Was it effective?

FIVE WAYS TO 'DRESS' FOR AUTUMN
(THE CONFLICTUAL STAGE)

1) Develop communication skills:

Healthy arguments involve being self-aware and reflective individuals who listens to understand. This require both parties being vulnerable and discussing the matter rather than arguing or circling around it. Inevitably, your communication skills will be tested. It is important to develop conflict resolution strategies to ensure matters do not escalate and voices are heard. (TIPS: do not ignore conflict - kip it in the bud as soon as you recognise them, identify a solution after both parties have shared their grievances, and of course, apply the Argyle's communication cycle model).

2) Attend relationship seminars/retreat or listen to relationship podcast together:

Attending seminars or couples retreat will award both parties the practical tools and space to strengthen their relationship. Individuals may even meet other couples experiencing similar issues and benefit from sound advice.

3) Continue going on dates:

Although this may seem like the last thing on your mind, prioritising date nights enables both parties to de-stress and rekindle old flames.

4) Couple therapy:

This will enable you to gain a new and deeper perspective regarding your relationship from a trained professional. What are your communication patterns? How do you both handle conflict? How can you restore trust? What do you love about each other?

5) Pray:

Prayers can help restore broken relationships. Remember, the enemy hates love and would do anything to divide individuals. It is your duty to recognise this and pray against it.

FIVE WAYS TO 'PROTECT' YOURSELF DURING AUTUMN

1) Avoid passive aggressive behaviours – silent treatment:

This form of 'punishment' is abusive and detrimental to the health of a relationship. It is a manipulation tactic that can leave important issues in a relationship unresolved. Emotional distance is a way to inflict pain without leaving a physical bruise. It leaves the partner on the receiving end feeling hurt, confused, and insignificant. It also communicates a clear message that the perpetrator does not care enough to work things out.

2) Uproot the weed of mistrust:

It is not enough to make verbal declarations in attempt to get your partner to trust you. The remedy for mistrust is not found in promising, 'I will never do it again.' Words are meaningless when trust is eroded. It is not a love issue. You cannot say, 'if you love me, you will trust me.' And it is certainly not a forgiveness issue. You can still forgive someone but not trust them. The true remedy to restore trust is to simply be a trustworthy person. Let your actions speak louder than your words.

3) Self-reflect:

Developing self-reflection and awareness is a key step to cultivating healthier relationships. It opens doors for true intimacy, vulnerability, and openness. You can identify areas of development within self, take accountability and apologise if needed.

4) Avoid letting pride and ego tarnish what you have

Pride can be a destructive force in a relationship. Not being able to take accountability and apologise communicates immaturity and alienates you from your loved one.

5) It is important to look at the bigger picture

Getting a big picture perspective allows you both to reinforce the things that are important and subsequently refocus your attention on what really matters.

For example, if your relationship goal is to build a loving family but you keep having petty arguments, it is time to reset your priorities. Are your arguments productive? If not, kip it in the bud and avoid dragging it.

As Tuckman mentioned, once you get over the dips in your relationship, you naturally progress to the *'norming'* stage (see below). During this stage, conflict is resolved, you begin to accept each other's flaws and realise you are a team aiming for a common goal.

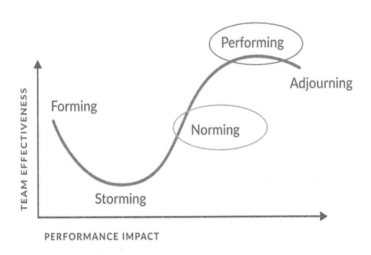

From looking at the diagram above, feelings and emotions begin to increase. In fact, your relationship reaches a deeper level of understanding and intimacy.

It is at its peak! This is the final stage where you have both proven to each other that you care and are committed. As the relationship continues to blossom, couples progress to the *'performing'* stage. Arguably, this is the stage where men fall deeper in love. Women tend to fall back into their femininity and submits wholeheartedly to her partner. He has proven to have the qualifications to 'fly' her 'plane' without crashing it. Congratulations! It is not easy to get to this stage. It requires a lot of patience, vulnerability, endurance, forgiveness and commitment.

Relationship Inventory

Since transparent conversations are nothing new in your relationship, it should be easier to have intimate discussions surrounding your recent fall.

The outcome of your conversation should be centred on pulling the weeds that strangled your relationship. These innocuous weeds can ruin your garden if left ignored.

The weeds of disrespect, selfishness, and pride needs to be uprooted during the relationship inventory (if not, daily) before they grow into stubborn twigs. Presumably, this explains why some couples have trouble moving pass the same argument. They did not pay vigilant care to their garden and allowed their weeds to grow.

To stay on topic, the relationship inventory not only allows you to discuss your weeds but allows you both to replant your seeds and nourish your garden. In practical sense, this looks like revisiting your boundaries, communicating your conflict style, and finding new ways to cater to each other.

My Story

From experience, conflict resolution has been successful in learning more about each other's needs, reviewing the contract and discovering ways to manage conflict. This enabled myself and my partner to grow as a couple - making the relationship fruitful.

On the contrary, I have been in situations, where conflict was dealt with using the silence tactic. Silence is the lowest form of communication. It communicates a deep message that something is wrong. This gives birth to assumptions. According to Henry Winkler, "assumptions are the termites of relationships. It can grow and manifest - deepening insecurities and unnecessary hurt". Moreover, assumptions can alter people's perceptions of reality. Behaviours then become modified based on incorrect information. To avoid this, frank conversations needs to be had.

In Summary:

• Conflict is an inevitable part of a relationship. It is a testing ground to discover your conflict style as a couple.

• Effective communication and prayers are the ingredients that holds couples together.

• Arygle's 'communication cycle' model teaches couples how to develop effective communication even in the most challenging circumstances.

• Silent treatments are manipulative tactics that can damage relationships.

• Once you overcome your 'relationship roadblocks', your relationship would elevate to the next level – making it meaningful.

11

WINTER (THE ROCKY STAGE)

ust when things were going well, you are suddenly approached with thunder, lightning or even snow! Temperatures begins to get cold. The weather looks gloomy, and outside is grim.

It appears as though there is always one thing after another. Unlike before, you are *both* equally invested. In fact, *both* souls are connected to the point that you do not want to give up. At the same time, you cannot help but notice another dip in your relationship. This is the *winter* stages of a relationship.

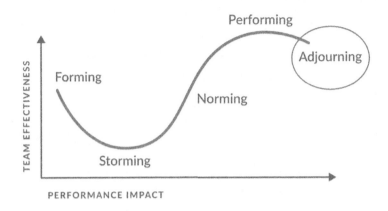

Tuckman mentioned people during this stage are prepared to say goodbye. They reflect on their relationship journey and realise it may be best to depart. There is a sudden realisation that their relationship has come to an end. The contract has terminated. Both parties may mourn over the loss.

However, this is not always the case. If you continue to dress according to the weather and apply the same strategies you used during the 'storming' stage, you would be able to revert back to the 'performing' phase of your relationship. Remember, after winter comes spring! However, this may take a lot of patience, tears, and commitment. But like the seasons, this too shall past. Your situation has an expiry date. It just requires a change of mindset. What do I mean by this? Even though you are experiencing winter in your home, it does not need to be cold! You can both put the heater on or grab a blanket. The point made is; you need to actively respond to the temperature change by applying innovative ways to dress for the weather. Not to mention, the receipe for Love (see page 1).

FIVE WAYS TO 'DRESS' FOR WINTER
(THE ROCKY STAGE)

1) Give each other space:

Experts say it is easier to revive a broken relationship with space. Space in a relationship does not mean it has ended. Rather, it allows both parties to pay closer attention to their emotions and reconnect in a healthy way. In addition, too much interference can create friction. If you live and breathe each other, little teething issues will start to annoy you. Time apart allows partners to miss and value each other and the relationship.

2) Go on holiday together:

Once you have provided each other with appropriate space, you may wish to book a holiday together. Escapism is important because it helps you both to unwind and reignite sparks that made your relationship work so well in the beginning. Recent studies suggest couples who travel together, stay together. You can disconnect from the outside world and reconnect internally.

3) Communicate:

Relationships require a deep level of emotional intelligence. In this case, it is not about who is right or who is wrong. Communicate your needs and feelings. This should never lead to an argument. Irrespective of whether you are hurt or angry, you must be mindful of your tone. Most people switch off when spoken to in an attentive or rude manner. The receiver becomes defensive and fixated on the delivering rather than the message (it takes a lot of patience and skill for someone to bypass that).

4) Couple therapy:

Consider returning to the same therapist. They already understand the patterns and dynamics of your relationship journey and are usually happy to help.

5) Pray and fast:

Prayers and fasting can help restore broken relationships. Remember, the enemy hates love and would do anything to divide individuals. It is your duty to recognise this and fast against it.

FIVE WAYS TO 'PROTECT' YOURSELF DURING WINTER

1) Avoid speaking out of emotions:

When you are hurt, you say hurtful things. Hurtful words can be irreversible. Most people throw insults to express temporary pain. Your pain has an expiry date, your words do not.

When anger creeps you, it is best to take your frustration to God. Let God deal with the person – not you.

2) Avoid empty threats:

If you do not want to break up, don't say it. These impulsive decisions are emotionally abusive habits which can push a person away.

In addition, making threats can back you into a corner and make you feel obligated to follow it through, even though you don't want to.

3) Avoid seeking attention from the opposite sex:

Emotional or physical cheating can be the death sentence of a relationship. Studies found anxiously attached partners are more likely to cheat. This is because they seek closeness from others and become dissatisfied when they do not receive it from their partner. Arguments in a relationship can communicate to the anxious person that their partner will abandon them. As a result, they gravitate towards anyone that will provide them with love, attention, and intimacy they so desperately crave.

4) Avoid prolonging space in your relationship:

Although space can revive broken relationships too much space can be equally detrimental. It opens doors for the enemy to plant seeds of doubts, insecurities, and temptations.

5) Pray:

Pray this prayer: 'Father in heaven, You brought my partner and me together. That is why I boldly come before Your throne and ask that You heal our relationship. There has been so much hurt caused by arguments, pride, and insecurities. I ask that you let this relationship be guided by love and not by our selfish interest. Amen.

Relationship Inventory

If after trying to make things work, you both realise it is time to terminate the contract, a conversation needs to be had. You have been mulling over the same issues and despite putting the *heater* on, you are both *cold*. In fact, temperatures within your relationship are beyond freezing!

During this stage, individuals may be tempted to walk away or even send a text without having a final talk. This is irresponsible. According to Jonathan Bennet (a relationship and dating expert) breakups should involve a lot of thought and communication – 'it's only fair to your partner that you are open and transparent'.

During the relationship inventory, you can get things off your chest and have a final honest assessment of your situation. You can explore your relationship journey together and evaluate the pros and cons of your relationship. Both parties will then be in a better position to arrive at an amicable decision and go their separate ways.

Although breakup conversations are never easy, it communicates respect and maturity. It also allows the relationship to dissolve in peaceful terms with closure. If it ends abruptly, it can spark bitterness, confusion, and resentment. Of course, this is subjective to the relationship and the reason behind the breakup.

Nonetheless, you may both decide to give the relationship another shot. This is because effective communication has an interesting way of bringing people closer together (when done the right way).

This time, you vow to continue watering your garden with love, care, and attention. When you both reach this mutual decision, you realise relationships has many seasons. The aim is to identify which season you are in and dress accordingly! Typically, once you have experienced all the seasons, you will be more equipped in discerning when the weather is about to change and do something about it.

My Story

I broke up mentally before physically walking out of my five-year relationship. My partner and I would constantly argue over nothing. My fuse with him was short.

During our relationship inventory, we realised it was best to depart. Upon reflection, that was the best decision we made. Now, we maintain an amicable relationship.

Had we ended abruptly, either via "ghosting" or via text, we may of had unresolved anger, hurt and bitterness towards each other – leading to karmic relationships.

In Summary:

• Relationship goes through a series of ups and downs.

• When a relationship compromises your mental health, it is best to leave.

• During a disagreement, release your frustration to God not each other. You can't take your words back.

• When breaking up seems to be the only solution, the most respectable way to deal with it is in person (rather than ghosting or sending a text). This provides a nice closure to your relationship journey and each leave with a good reputation.

CONCLUSION

R elationships are a beautiful thing and comes from God. It is His intention that His creations have fruitful and productive relationships. For this reason, Love is embedded within our DNA.

The Bible describes Love as 'patient' and 'kind'. We must therefore display these attributes towards our loved ones. Of course, it is easy to display 'patience' and 'kindness' during the beginning stages of a relationship when things are cosy but what about when things get rocky? This is the time when our faith is tested.

Remember, the enemy despise Love so will orchestrate events to cause doubts, confusion, and heartbreaks. That is why it is imperative to invite God at the conceptual stages of your relationship.

Your insecurities stemming from childhood traumas or past relationships are key events the enemy can use to sabotage relationships. Therefore, regular self-assessment, healing and self-love are required before entering a relationship.

Thank you for reading this book. I hope you find it useful, practical and informative! It is my aim to promote healthy, long-lasting and deserving relationships whilst identifying signs of toxic situations.

If you feel triggered by the content of this book or you are trapped in a cycle of abuse, please seek prayer and formal support.

Alternatively, if you have applied some of the strategies or would like to share your thoughts and opinions, feel free to leave a comment using our app.

Wishing you a lovely day and most importantly a fruitful relationship 😊

Guide to Support Options for Abuse

Taking the first step in seeking help for abuse can feel difficult. You may especially feel this way if you have tried to talk to friends, family or professionals and have not had a response that helped you.

This page list organisations and services who may be able to offer you support for abuse. Help is available whether you're experiencing abuse now or have done in the past.

Find details of support options for:

1. SAMARITANS
116 123 (freephone)
jo@samaritans.org

Samaritans are open 24/7 for anyone who needs to talk. You can visit some Samaritans branches in person. Samaritans also have a Welsh Language Line on 0808 164 0123 (7pm–11pm every day).

2. VICTIM SUPPORT
0808 168 9111
victimsupport.org.uk
Provides emotional and practical support for people affected by crime and traumatic events.

3. The National Association for People Abused in Childhood (NAPAC)
0808 801 0331
support@napac.org.uk

napac.org.uk
Supports adult survivors of any form of childhood abuse. Offers a helpline, email support and local services.

4. One in Four
0800 121 7114
oneinfour.org.uk
Offers advocacy services, counselling, and resources for adults who have experienced trauma, domestic or sexual abuse in childhood.

5. SAFER PLACES
0330 102 5811
saferplaces.co.uk
Helpline, a live chat and information for adults who have experienced domestic and sexual abuse or violence. Offers refuge accommodation services in Essex and Hertfordshire.

6. MEN'S ADVICE LINE
0808 801 0327
mensadviceline.org.uk
Confidential advice and support for men who have experienced domestic violence and abuse by a current or ex-partner or family member.

Printed in Great Britain
by Amazon

24135500R00077